Margaret Hasse

STARS ABOVE, STARS BELOW

STARS ABOVE

STARS BELOW

Margaret Hasse

Graphics by Mike Lynch

Minnesota Voices Project #19

New Rivers Press 1984

Book Design: Daren Sinsheimer and C. W. Truesdale
Typesetting: Peregrine Cold Type
Back Cover Photograph: Timothy Francisco

Some of the poems in this book have previously appeared in the following publi-
cations: *142 Ways to Make a Poem* (anthology), *Dacotah Territory, Mid-
American Review, 25 Minnesota Poets #2* (anthology), *The Lake Street Review,
WARM Journal, Fresh Air* (a magazine of KFAI Radio), *Milkweed Chronicle,
Moons and Lion Tailes, Sunbury, The Great Circumpolar Bear Cult, A Change in
Weather: Midwest Women Poets* (anthology), *Great River Review, Northeast,
Horizons: The South Dakota Writers' Anthology,* and *Border Crossings*
(anthology). Our thanks to the editors of these publications for permission to
reprint here.

The author would like to thank friends and family for their love and support, and
to express gratitude to her teachers, especially those who taught English and en-
couraged her to write. Deborah Keenan's smart, generous editing improved
Stars Above, Stars Below. Publisher Bill Truesdale was also an excellent person
to work with. Paulette Bates Alden, Jim Moore, Jill Breckenridge, Margot Kriel,
Don Brunnquell, Patricia Hampl, Michael Hazard, Roy McBride, Susan Welch,
and Gary Egger helped by critiquing individual poems or reviewing the
manuscript.

Stars Above, Stars Below was published with the aid of grants from the Jerome
Foundation, the Dayton Hudson Foundation (with funds provided by B. Dalton,
Bookseller), the United Arts Council (with funds provided in part by the Mc-
Knight Foundation), the First Bank System Foundation, and the Metropolitan
Regional Arts Council (with funds appropriated by the Minnesota State
Legislature.)

New Rivers Press books are distributed by

       Small Press Distribution   Bookslinger
       1784 Shattuck Ave.   213 E. 4th St.
       Berkeley, CA 94709   St. Paul, MN 55101

Stars Above, Stars Below has been manufactured in the United States of America
for New Rivers Press, Inc. (C. W. Truesdale, Editor/Publisher), 1602 Selby Ave.,
St. Paul, MN in a first edition of 1000 copies.

Stars Above, Stars Below
is dedicated to the memory of my mother and my father
and the observatory in Vermillion, South Dakota.

Going back I realized the picnic was for us. It started
raining in a totally different way, knowing we'd grow
right on up into wars and trains and deaths and loving
people and leaving them and being alone.

—James L. White from "An Ordinary
Composure" in *The Salt Ecstasies*

STARS ABOVE, STARS BELOW

STARS ABOVE, STARS BELOW

I. THE GARDEN AT DUSK

We had finished trimming the tree.
Lying on a braided rug
after the family had gone to bed
in the dark rooms
I knew each shadow of,
I was a little girl up too late,
and growing later.

The tree lights were off
like jewels suddenly missing,
my father first,
then later many I loved.

I remembered how
the most beautiful tree
won Jesus' heart
and he gave to those who decorated it
his everlasting attention.

Limb by needled limb
I wanted to climb the evergreen
like an unfamiliar stair
toward the top star,
the one which was a heart
that knew how to stay put.

She's a quiet clapper in the bell of the prairie,
a girl who likes to be alone.
Today, she's hiked four miles down
ravines' low cool blueness.
Bending under a barbed wire, she's in grass fields.
She's at the edge of the great plains.
Wise to openness, she finds it a familiar place.
Her clothes swell like wheat bread.

When she returns to her parents' house,
the foxtails and burrs have come home, too.
The plants seem intent on living in new ground.
She's the carrier. "Carrier" is a precision
learned in summer's biology class.
She likes to think of ripening seeds,
a cargo inside the bellies of flying birds.
Birds like red-winged blackbirds who skim the air
and land, alert on their cattail stalks.
They allow her a silent manner.
They go about their red-winged business
of crying to each other, dipping their beaks
into the swampy stand of ditch water,
full of the phantom of green.
The stiller she is, the more everything moves
in the immense vocabulary of being.

We've returned to autumn
leaving summer a clear lake on which lilies float.
We are back from the season of light,
of lying in warm grass and watching clouds fly;
we're back from a time of round birds,
flagrantly yellow.

Summer still remains in my hair.
Hands sometimes hold sleek water.
There is the sweet cider of apples in store
and two combs of honey on the shelf.

Now the apples on the tree are faces,
the porch light is out,
and we huddle behind our separate doors.

We come back to autumn,
to zucchini that wilt like witches' shoes,
to games of solitaire at night,
to silence in the wake of snow geese
which pass high overhead
and empty our mouths with their cries.

—after a theme of Seferis

You are home town.
You are all my favorite places
the last summer I grew up.
Every once in a while
I write you
in my head
to ask how Viet Nam
and a big name college
came between us.
We tried to stay in touch
through the long distance,
the hum and fleck of phone calls.

It was inevitable
that I should return
to the small prairie town
and find you
pumping gas, driving a truck, measuring lumber,
and we'd exchange
weather talk,
never be able to break through words
and time to say simply:
"Are you as happy
as I wanted you to be?"

And still I am stirred
by musky cigarette smoke
on a man's brown suede jacket.
Never having admitted the tenderness
of your hands, I feel them now
through my skin.
Parking on breezy nights,
in cars, floating passageways,
we are tongue and tongue like warm cucumbers.

I would walk backwards
along far country roads
through late evenings, cool as moving water,
heavy as red beer,
to climb into that August.

In the dark lovers' lanes,
you touched my face
and found me here.

In the grid of her stanchion, the oldest cow chews at a regular rhythm as if she were listening privately to a tune she liked. She turns slowly to look at him; whiskers of hay drip from her mouth. Her nostrils are mossy black; her eyes sleepy and wet. She turns away. Her puffed udder is pink with a tracing of the whitest albino hairs. The ancient-looking teats, stretched long as fingers.

She won't be budged by the pain of a full bag into accepting the new milking machines. So he sits on a tri-legged stool and strokes milk into the crown of an aluminum pail. His cheek against the broad flank where a whirlpool of hair begins its soft reversal. His ear to that clock, his hands about the business of pulling sweet, necessary milk into use.

I wanted Daniel but he didn't want me.
He wanted my friend Patricia,
who wasn't a pompom girl,
but wore her skirts short anyway.
Over cherry Cokes served in tulip glasses,
we decided that upperclassmen
leave you lonely.
But when he called
to ask her to be his date
at the Homecoming Prom,
her answer was an eager "Yes."

That Friday we won the big game
and Daniel danced close to Patricia,
braiding his arms around her.
Her black dress-up dress cupped
her seat with satin.
"Moon River" crooned out
of the record player as glitter
began to flake from the streamers
above the gym floor, falling
like silver dust on the couples below.

They drove the borrowed car
directly into the country,
parking west of town.
October's cool edge kept
the heater running.
Their mouths spun candied
webs of moisture.
The huge hulk of the Chevrolet
held their damp and yearning bodies,
darkness within darkness.
While exhaust poured blue
beyond the backseat,
stars fell slowly out of the sky.
And in the early morning,
the motor stopped running.

Downtown Saturday noon,
Connie Sorenson whispered
that they found them—
still, embracing.
They say it doesn't hurt
and that you never know
it's not air you're breathing.

We're in the bottom of the swimming pool
in September after they've pulled the plug.
Now the only blue is the paint
loose in large patches like eczema,
and Craig Kaiser is calling my name
from over in the deep end.

Boys' soft tongues, hard hands
begged us to let go, and our bodies
wanted to shout back, swim in over our heads.
But in 1965, the campaign on the side
of not letting go was tremendous.

Our mothers enlisted their large words
speaking of menstruation and marital bonds,
of brassieres worn like life jackets,
making all things more formal
so that they belonged not to us,
but to those small town hens
who cackled over our virginity.

In school the film for girls only
confirmed our bodies would condemn us,
our sins balloon and live forever.
Born out of control, the unwanted ghost:
a face lost to the family album.
Some of the boys learned this too,
peeking through slices of light that fell
into the black room where we sat,
hot packages under wraps.

THE EVENING NEWS

Five-thirty would find my father
in his favorite chair,
legs crossed, one slipper dangling,
thumbs in their gyrations.
Everything still and within reach:
T.V. tray with dinner,
reading light and books,
child's head,
the television, its tempting light.

We watch Walter Cronkite's show.
Walter brings the world home
and my father helps us learn to live with it.
It is just awful to see both men cry
especially when Jackie Kennedy does not.
My father scrunches the doilies
on the chair's arms and moans:
"Our President, our President,"
with an odd trembling in an outward calm.

Even though Walter tells us news
of tornadoes and bad weather,
of small bodies being carried
from a bombed church,
we know he does not want to.
We know he hated Viet Nam.

His program is in color now,
his dark hair silver,
his suit a plain brown.
He coughs now; we worry about him.

When he goes off the air,
there will be no one to trust,
to watch dissolve into unreal oranges,
into blues that are not true
but hold us anyway.

Odin's farm lay at the end
of a quarter mile dirt road.
From a distance, the house and barn
wavered in the heat like Oz.
We arrived on ponies, the place
between saddle and back lathered
white as cake frosting.
If we shouted into the lapping rows,
Odin might come out of the fields,
pushing the leaves aside
like strands of long hair
and cradling ears of perfect corn.
He'd show us around,
stupefied by our company,
joyous as a puppy.
Odin was musty as a basement.
We loved his singular magic
and lands free to us as air.
His chickens were loose change
in the yard; pigs slept
their fatty sleep in his garden.
The old buck rabbit in his separate cage
lying bored on his side,
panting and stinky.
The he-goats, too, emitted a cheesiness
we didn't recognize.

Once, after a scolding
about old, odd men and their loneliness,
we did notice that the zipper's teeth
in his trousers were sharp
and silver and wide-open,
and our mothers' words made us feel
creepy and wrong.
So we stuck our whole heads
into the trough where his catfish

cast quick and slippery shadows
on the bottom, where the artesian
water's cold shocked us back up
into the sunlight with lips
as slim and blue as fish's.

A girl sits alone in her mother's house
and eats a bowl of ice cream and then another.
Her prospects are bleak.
The sleeves of her dress cut a line across her flesh.
It is uncomfortable to sit in your body
in well-made clothes and feel desperately hugged.
That is why she eats ice cream
knowing as she does that it won't do any good.
A size is what you cut out of air.
Rumpled and round, she cuts hers out of yards,
wraps air around her in a pale pink nubbiness
and sits in its center.

It is her bowl of ice cream although her mother
bought it and has gone out of the house
hiding the brownies in a back closet.
When the girl was a very little girl
and the family lived together,
she would say to her daddy:
"And what cookie is mine?"
And he would say back in a rounded "O" manner
as he was told to speak to children:
"The one with your name on it,"
and she knew she could eat every one on the platter.

The girl leaves her bowl on the thesaurus
where she's been looking up synonyms for perfection,
and ferrets out the brownies,
seeking to be full, to fill herself
with anything she can get her hands on.

When my mother
smelling of milk and bread
brushes the long robe of my hair,
the vines spring roses.
We wake in a white bed
floating with feather pillows.
Morning patterns her face.
She curls me in her arms;
she is a seashell,
white and full of song.

And now I come to tuck
my little mother into bed.
I am too young to be empty-armed
and the weeds in my throat
will not let me sing lullabies.

Waiting has teeth in it.

My mother smiles at me
and wraps around herself.
I won't see her cry;
her wheat body does not even shake.
She will not know
how the echoes return.
Silent tears are turquoise
peacock feathers which tickle
and the hyena in me laughs,
crazy, crazy.

And my mother
on her thin shelved bed
hears the dogs move restlessly.
There is a clack of their nails
on linoleum.
She knows they have come for her.
She whimpers, they whimper.

Soon there will be no one
to tell me what I was like
when I was a child.

—My mother said to me,
"You slipped out of me so easily,
just like a wish."

There are dandelion lanterns all about
but mostly in the morning they shine.
I love their pretty lights,
that beauty around me.

There used to be a field near us
where those lights glittered and shone.
I could reach them and kiss them.

When your mother dies
I bet she will be happy
if you pick them
and put them in your heart
and send them up to her.
And tie your name tag to them.
I know she'll have you in her heart.
I know you love her.
I love mine.
So pick your gold lights.
It's time you sent them up
to her and god.

—written in 1957

I have seen her dying.
Sometimes she is shaking in my arms,
sometimes she is stretched on a thin white pallet.

To imagine her death over and over
is to find myself where breath begins
except I am awake, falling
in space with the stars counted as lost souls.

It's too bad that things don't happen just once.
Each time it is different from before.
I see a new angle of despair:
an elbow akimbo,
a kneecap poking weed-like
out of the flat skeleton.

Her eyes open out of a watchful face.
Shapes approach.
For her we are all the same.
She was afraid of me
when I tiptoed in at midnight
to take her pulse,
stroke a stray hair
from her forehead.

"Even hair is scarce," she said.
Then: "I am going. I am going."
Dry lips move about her mouth,
a small dark hole that descends
into the earth and beyond.

Little gold lights
with strings tied to your bottoms,
I like you.
I pick you every day
for my mama.
I like you, little gold lights
with strings.
Good night.
You will die
on a windy, windy day.
Gold lights. Good night.

—written in 1955

There are many ways of saying goodbye:
the single flip of a wrist, sent flowers,
a note nudged between door and screen.

Some goodbyes take years to make.
Articulated, you keep using them
in slow repetitions of your story.

This chapter's set at a pitstop,
somewhere in Nevada, half-way to a new home.
A Greyhound bus idles its motor
like a stunned animal trying to catch its breath.
You've held yourself apart
from the other passengers
who open and close the door of the cafe
in bright bombs of color.
At the boundary of the neon flash,
the desert begins.
Silhouettes of cactus razor stroke the dawn.
Apricot rises, rolling up a blue shade.
All this you make yourself notice.
You believe you're a thoughtful young woman
on the edge of something.

At the other end of night, its beginning,
you were in Omaha, Nebraska,
the city you called escape.
You gave your family the slip.
They waved from the bus dock
as if nothing had happened.

Your mind runs its giant hand
along the land, sweeps over the Rockies,
returns to where your home town sleeps,
your one and single town.
Under a dark dome, houses set out
as on a monopoly board.

Your family each in their tiny beds
and you too big for them now.

Your sleepy eyes smart in the chill air.
Stars float in their own deep liquid.
Your arms are full of bumps
from the cold, and what's never behind.

We've avoided each other
for six years, since the last funeral.
Now, together, we have nothing to cry about,
no one memory
to focus affection and history,
no mother, no father.
It makes us restless.

I go to the bar to drink beer with my nephews.
Two sisters stay home and play word games.
Another sticks close to her husband.
My brother takes his boat to the water,
urging us all to have a good time.

At night, the water laps monotonously.
We wake, cranky. Two more days to go.

That evening, family picture night.
First we are the upside-down family bats
hanging around a picnic feast.
Once we're righted, the camera's eye
flies about, up in the trees during the wedding part
where the bride is supposed to come out of the church.
All we get is ankles and grass,
then neighbors and friends dimly remembered.

Aided by adult hands,
we each take first steps in these pictures.
We cut our hair for the military.
Someone gave us away. We get married.
Brothers get sprayed by hoses,
sisters hold babies now in college,
students sitting beside me in the room.

A film we've been waiting for without knowing it existed:
after three minutes of flowers and backyards
that aren't even pretty,

there they are, standing by a blue Rambler,
our mother, our father, stars in the film
which pauses on them, wavers,
wants to move away,
stays still for ten seconds, more.
My sister provides the subtitles:
"There he is, back from the hospital,
Iowa City, the baby's not born yet,
look how beautiful mother's hair is, even then."

Green light mottles them
like ivy covering and crumbling
the face of the childhood house.
The reel runs out, keeps turning,
and we stay still in the room,
a family gathered
against the nick, nick at the film's end.

All spring we have been waiting for rain.

In the sweat shops of the sheets
our bodies curl like drought grubs.
The commas of our shapes
punctuate the dusty distances
between what we hope for and can have.

Our nights must evolve into more
than bad dreams of heat.

Farmers' spittle sows the fields.
Dry land cannot confess its green.
Bread cannot rise out of its brown nurseries.

Cracked terracotta, our lips
are unsealed by need and we speak
of stripping down to essential love.

It is very late.
From the dark, thunder confirms
the unknown others.

Weather too hot for touch we say.
Lightning the only torch.

I walk to the car parked
on a dark side street.
I'm a hand of solitaire,
someone a bully could pick off.
I fidget with the keys.
A jogger is not dark Mercury
delivering a message about health.

Home for five minutes all alone,
the call comes,
the one with only breathing.

The time the plane sank
and the cups jumped
and the little woman next to me
melded into my shoulder,
the right words rose to my tongue
like spit: "there, there."

I always was the brave one,
taking the dark walk alone.
The city pool, after lights out,
a skimmed bowl.
Chlorine glittered everywhere.
"It's O.K.," to the girls
in their two piece suits,
"you go on together, I'm fine."
I marched by mailboxes
silvery in the farm yardlights.

The corn that guarded
the left closed in.
Trees grew in fisted woods
on both sides of the road bank.
I paused, a dammed stream.
The road, one line of white dashes,
something left unsaid.

Later we did say
that patch of road
was "hell's own soul."

Sixth graders, we scared ourselves
just saying the words.
I still do:
the darkness of hell,
the hugeness of soul.

II. SECRETS AND RUMORS

INCIDENT

We found her on our side stoop
like a stray animal, wincing
under the attention of our car lights.
While we waited for action
to occur to us, she assembled
her confusion slightly
and vanished down the road
towards the railroad tracks
where I've seen people
wrapped in leaves, sleeping.

The moon carved up the backyard
into pieces.
We walked to the edge of the lilac,
looked up to the stars, each one
polished and well-placed.
Except the ones whose fall
announce their failing beauty
with a brief white scar.

At thirteen she begins having fainting spells.
All indoor places are suspect,
especially churches.
The voice of the minister calls a blush
to her pale arms.
He is reading from St. Paul, and badly.

Her imperturbable mother tongues
the back sides of her teeth.
She knows the signs.
She is glad for an excuse to remember
how sparks once flew
from the touch of everything.

Morning, and the world looks brand-new
as if all its windows had been washed.
The girl rises
and steps into her body.
She has decided to wear it
for the rest of her life.

1.

He wakes with a start.
Something missing: woman,
money, watch, gun.
It's like a face tic, this
desire to feel the cool green
cubes of dice.
His mama wished some real
good woman would come along,
keep him out of jail.

2.

"He called today," my housemate says.
Certain pronouns are so personal
you always know who's behind the word.
"It sounded as if there were children
in the background."
As they jostle in line for the phone,
prisoners have been mistaken
for a class of kindergarteners.

3.

Tonight all women who love him
stand at windows thinking Christmas.
He begs me—speaking from the blind eye
of a telephone—to snap a picture
of my tree, because he remembers
I've never been home at Christmas before.

The picture I'll send,
with ornaments in clusters:
a herd of small horses,
and high in the slope of branches,
a band of angels—those mountain climbers—

the incarnation in miniature
of the imperial ghosts which take
our loneliness under the span
of their ageless wings tonight
and gamble with it for his redemption.

Not much he asks for: simply a room
with two windows for a cross breeze.
A bed to fall down on.
And neighbors who don't inquire.

He is the bridegroom of restlessness.
He who can stay only a month
in a rented room, furnished.
One job, one city, one friend.
One star will grace him
in the one window of one large house
where the smell of ancient oil
makes his room a cage.
Where people exist
as angry voices through the walls.

THE MAN IN THE GRASS

What rots first on the man in the grass?

First his eyes, in the manner
of roadside squirrels',
their sockets alive with black flies,
their interminable cleaning.

Second, the mouth, its useless channel,
the air buzzing all around him in May,
his lungs lax and flattened.

Then the stillness of the stomach
and genitals, paper bags
in the warm rain of June.

In July, his clothes separate
in relaxed threads,
cotton a delicate web
as if modesty were a bad thing
in the bulbed eyes of the sun.

In our civilized world it is rare
that a man can melt down in a slow airy progress.
This body, one short fall from the bone
when a runner steps off the trail,
sees a shred he thinks at first is a nest.

The runner is unfamiliar with the ways
of dead bodies,
hasn't been a witness
to their grim and holy return.
Closer now, he emits a giant moan.

When Michael wants to cry
he slides into the solace of water.
Sand falls down the eye of an hourglass.
Pushing on through the tiny hole
that grief permits a man,
he swims toward his tears.

From the catch of blue sea shadows,
he escapes again and again,
stretching his arms in free-style cries.

An arrow shaft woven
in gossamer wet of skin and sorrow,
he slips out of dozens of shapes
which dissolve behind him in fierce flutter kicks.

Michael is chasing after
sad swift animals that live in his eyes.

One a.m. in the warehouse district.
The men are taking a break on the loading dock.
Irv, Danny, Frank: they have hands
like welders' mitts. Frank unwraps
damp wax paper from a sandwich as four women
come out of a building across the street.
"The scenery keeps getting better and better,"
Danny shouts. The women laugh
and the laughter carries back to the men
a prickling sense of adventure.
The women are leaving a party, stepping out
under huge fluorescent lights.

The men live with a quiet density
no one thinks about.
Irv will go home at 6 a.m.
and wake up Loretta, his high school girl,
and send her off to school
with a good breakfast.
He doesn't talk much and his daughter sometimes
yells at his silence, wants him to tell jokes
like her boyfriends' fathers.

One of the women climbing into the old Plymouth
across the street looks like Loretta's mother—
the cut of her curly dark hair.
Irv moves a little in his chair.
Now the others are whistling and stomping.
He feels slightly religious, as if he has entered
a big room as a child.

Nikos comes from Greece.
An American woman wants to help, marries him.
They begin having screaming arguments.
He is not a citizen, but married to her—
all right—he can stay.
Stay in New York, stay in Chicago,
stay in San Francisco.

At Athena's, at Minerva's,
at all the bars and tavernas
scattered along Eddy Street,
he dances like a riot.

He tells mariners' stories:
"And yes, the cold so cold we breathed
a bit of our own death."
He teaches women the simple words
that are in English similar to the Greek:
astro, philos, prophylactic.

In every song, there's a little story
of a love and the myriad ways
it can go wrong. It can go wrong
as she stands in the kitchen
frying eggs; it can go wrong
as he's driving truck
through slick black nights,
down highways too long to dream about.
It can go wrong
for a strike breaker or a star gazer.
It can break up with a word, a blow,
a night spent alone, over a T.V. show,
a menu, a baby who comes
or one who was only dreamed about.
Love, the country singer insists,
is the only thing worth anything.
The heart like a rock in the sand.
The waves in human song
break over it, over it.

As we enter the cafe
through the screen door
we feel stranger
than we really are.
The screed of a ceiling fan
stirs the heat and hamburger smells
to a new thickness.
On the wall are pictures
made of rice and noodles.
Nearby a rack of posters selling
the 4th of July pancake feed.

The waitress wears a dress white
as the sun-dazed street outside.
She presses coffee on us
like a bit of good advice.
The little man and woman
in the booth near ours
dip into their orange sherbet
as if it were their lives.

NIGHT GAME AT PARADE STADIUM

You bump into a friend in the bleachers.
He's walked out on a bad movie
to sit in this second-rate field
watching the P.O. men beat the "Finks,"
a police team. It's that kind of night.

Professional ball players get power
from their buttocks.
Even these city league players of softball
have enormous hams.
The lights coat each man
with a perfection you could live with.

If you spent all night in the park,
the pleasure of the wind
would overcome exhaustion.
Or you could sleep
in the field of long grass
like a lost ball,
a home run.

When the game's over and lights are cut,
you think you see the shiny back of a coin.
It's only a cigarette package
but it's catching the stars
in its cellophane wrap.

A young couple, cautioned
to stay above the neckline, leaves small favors
below, hickies decorating the throat.

They kiss where the sun doesn't shine,
or the moon either, deep inside.
To the flavor of the voice.
To the mushroomy scent.

The lungs, liver, heart,
all organs and the internal time-keepers, pace-makers,
pituitary glands, isthmuses, islands,
red seas, bridges, plants, nebulae:

everything alive waits to be eaten.

Cleaning the mouth of the other,
teeth clacking together like silverware
in their velvet drawers,
they murmur: "I like the way you do that.
I like you. It feels so good
I want to die."

About this black moth that fumes
against my bathroom mirror:

About the orchid in the refrigerator,
its purple stain:

About the lump in her breast
growing like a grain of rice:

About the x-rays like a cloud map
of the north pole:

About the cells in her blood,
a late night knocking at the door:

About the lungs like wet sheep,
about the hair like cut weeds:

And about these knives crossed
in the drawer:

Your voice is the staccato
of a teletype machine.
Your woman friend in Iowa
has been left by her husband
with no talking about it.
You and I talk for several hours
over bread, jasmine tea.
Saturday morning.
I fiddle with a blue vase
and it shoots its stock of blue light
onto the walls, ceiling, floor,
then mottles your face.
You're crying as you remember
your own pain in being left
by a man.
The house became larger
and life a list of useless tasks.
You leaned back into any soft thing:
a sofa,
a May afternoon,
an album of whale songs.
Pain is outside of you now
like a part of the room.
He is not outside,
he never will be.
He is not only a lilt of cologne,
a beard on someone else
clipped just so.
He is not the pin he gave you,
not the soup with fish
he was good at making.
He is something you ate for a long time
that built your bones,
your blood, the Rapunzel hair
that you keep letting down
to let up the new life, the love.

Now that winter's half-way here,
leaves swirl coldly
and babies aren't seen much
except in the captivity of nurseries,
slumbering with their hands
drawn into roses.

Babies are unto themselves,
a little sub-culture, none of whom suspect
how many babies are being held
all over the world.

Babies escape slowly
from the little pens, the seatbelts,
the restraining arms.
It's brilliant. Few notice
how tricky babies are.
On occasion, an aunt might fix
a bee-bee sharp eye on the little one,
and fire: "My how you've grown."
The escaping baby feels very uncomfortable.

Babies enter the world wise and impeccable.
They leave their little prisons,
put nakedness in abeyance,
take on the clothes of the world,
spend a long time trying to locate
a perfect love which resembles
their first.

From time to time, they achieve glimpses.
As when an aging baby
late for a business appointment,
sits dreamily in his car,
cigarette's blue smoke
lingering in curlicues.
Before him, a large leaf

shoved by the windshield wipers, is waving.
Or when a woman who has never run
to breathlessness, does so.
She's not a baby anymore.
Amazed she does not burst,
she draws in large packages of air,
thinks of air as the new blood.

In trains, you're hurdled through the dark.
In cars, you're in small black pockets.
In planes, you are early angels.
Ships encourage you to dream.

The plane tips. The moon rises
over the shoulder of silver.

In a train you lean closer, body rocketing.
The windows toss back the slender room.
You feel intimate, sexual, archaic.

On a ship, you have games and space.
You have ballrooms and berths, pools and patios.
You have time to unfold your clothes.
You stand on the open deck for hours.

The bird hop-stumbles
across the forest of grass
our lawn is.
He seeks umbrellaed bushes,
the dark leafy places
at the edge of the yard.

He has fallen
from a pocket in a tree,
from the plump perfection
of his mother,
her halo of wings.

You follow him,
giant step by step,
knowing he cannot live
to share the night
with the neighboring cats.

You make a nest from rags
in a cardboard box.
You dig worms;
he downs them
like a small guzzler.
You pet the sheen on his back
with one large finger.

In the morning he is dead,
lost outside
his bundle of cloth.
A small thing
can make such silence.
You stand by the garage
for a long time.

STILL LIFE

Several of Nature's People
I know, and they know me—
I feel for them a transport
Of Cordiality—

But never met this Fellow
Attended, or alone
Without a tighter breathing
And Zero at the Bone—

—Emily Dickinson

He came across a dead cow,
a spotted shadow in the grass.
He stumbled over the carcass,
that monstrous quiet.
His new shoes bright against
the leathery prong of the cow's leg.

He photographed the body
in its daily stages of decay.
Its stamina for staying a corpse was tremendous.
It flattened slightly
to a wrinkled picnic rug
slung on the earth, forgotten.

The cow's shape was a disappearing zero,
a place he circled until he stood
at the very center of a photograph
where the dead animal
had weighed down the weeds.
A ripple ran across the anise and brome grass
like the flesh on someone
touched, then chilled.

THE TREE WHICH IS ALWAYS PRESENT

To praise is the whole thing! A man who can praise
comes toward us like ore out of the silences
of rock. His heart, that dies, presses out
for others a wine that is fresh forever.

—Rainer Maria Rilke, *Sonnets to Orpheus*

Raking leaves into piles so her children can jump in
she has forgotten they consider themselves too old
to act like puppies rumpling the heaps.
So the hot little fans she's placed together stay together
in a neatness she doesn't always abide.
The tree she adores. It shakes itself
and drops what isn't essential.
The tree is a tall tree; there're plenty of leaves.
The tree doesn't ask for much, produces these leaves each year.
What the sky gives in sun and water is enough.
Not like the greedy bushes, wilting dramatically
when the gardener is careless or carefree for two days.
Not like the lawn with its need for endless
preening and clipping, seeding and special watering care,
its need for people to stay off with respect,
its need for her on her hands and knees removing dandelions.
The tree is what describes her house:
"Second from the corner, one tree out front ..."
So she leans on her rake in the crisp applause of late fall,
thanking the tree, its simple cadence of bare branch.
Then thinks of summer when the tree's a single umbrella of shade
allowing her friends to sit like secrets on the porch,
saying how anything is possible, and it's true.

III. OPEN WINDOWS

It seems as if an alarm has been going off
for days. Now silence.
The rain continues to fall steadily.
My seed packets say that most of the plants
in my garden need thoroughly warm soil.
I pull my wool sweater warmer around me.
There is only one cookie left in the jar.
I say names out loud in the quiet room,
my own name, my mother's,
then the name of the man I love.
I hope the fish are biting for him up north.
I hope they will always bite and be fleshy and good.
I am sustained by the quiet of the long weekend.
I am grateful to be speaking to myself.
I like the sudden cold of June.
I stay inside. I am inside. I am Margaret.
I am in love and alone.
I light candles. Steam folds onto the inside
of the windows so that I can barely see the rain,
the wet slick streets, the mysterious
yellow globe of light in a neighbor's green room.
I think about movies of Japan.
I look out of myself for myself.
I do not like the thought of dying.
I am not afraid.
I carry solitude with me as a whole fruit.
I want an apple. I have an apple
corked by a tiny stem.

Driving below dark clouds
from the city,
headlights glancing off slick pavement,
I reach out to touch that hand
on the seatcover beside me.
It curls back into itself,
disappears into his lap.

Against the hunched car's windowpane
I press my nose.
The rain visits my cheek,
streams across my face.
I slide out to the hood.
Brine crystalizes
near my ears.
I charge the ship,
my head stuck out to sea,
bare the long way to my breasts.
Men in odd helmets run my deck
and bicker.

I will dock again
somewhere near Bloomington
not so eager to wipe my eyes,
unsnarl my hair,
to be told that I made a scene
and should control myself.

To sweat within the fabric of longing.
To try to assuage what will always thirst.

Spill your drink
and toss yourself like a sky message
across the face of a man.

An adult is forever
trying to disguise a sweet tooth
large as an elephant's tusk,
chiding the greed of the sneaky
child within: Now
grow up, eat peanuts
and other healthy snacks.
Stay away from candy bars
with milk-white centers
which give a round belly
to the little girl
who lives on love
of dumb divinity
and M & M's
and chocolate kisses.

Call the sweet stuff, "Sweetie."
Lick salt,
linger over flesh,
and relish the sort of pleasure
parents cannot give or withhold.
With another, do deep dances
between bed sheets, or by a fireplace
or in the open wilderness.

Sometimes, though, when alone
or rising to the surface of sleep,
a craving consumes the human.
Forming a circle that holds
the stomach as close as the heart,
she cries out: *Food is feeding emptiness.*
I am starving for myself.

We throw snowballs
as an early practice for the team.
Turned thirty, it is more difficult
this year to find my way back
to summery demands.
Winter pounds have been added
like a rippling sealskin coat
groomed late at night:
popcorn buttered yellow
and salted apples,
cake for anyone's birthday,
cookies made because
the house seemed cold.

I'm past the time when power
can be purchased as lipstick
or small bikinis,
when the chatter of supermarket magazines
can draw me in
with their proclamations
of the weeks remaining until
swimming suits.
They sell another diet
guaranteed to let me get light.
I toss a chocolate bar
into the silver basket like a score.
I have weight.
I can throw it around.

There are losses and then there are losses.
Some are nicks in the knee. Skimming down
between second and first base after a low ball,
you miss. Clown face. The game goes
topsy-turvy in its score. Later, walking home,
you stop to pick sand out of raw skin.
A new baby cries out a window. Inside,
a mother, face flushed, wishes summer were over.
The traffic from the baseball games in the park
coats her throat with dust, makes her restless
when the cries go up, a red confetti
in the hot evenings.

Most losses make little difference to anyone:
a note stepped on with spikes, later
picked out of the shoes in pieces, read:
"Darlene, I love you, Darrol."
You are lost then, wondering who
first said, "I love you,"
and why you can't remember,
though you imagine it, white, cool.
Imagination is the only splendid catch
of memory. You have a mother now
and perfect little love notes attached
all over your body in the form of kisses.
They make you better.

You could use some kisses now on your knee cap
where the skin is rose-colored, bumpy,
and where drops of red blood are starting
to make their stand against your losses.
While you continue home past all the open windows,
the loss itself is lost.

I wake you in the middle of the night asking you the meaning of the word in my dream. We often ask each other vocabulary words and we have a dictionary, red, heavy, always open somewhere in the house. Five paperback dictionaries, smaller, brief in their descriptions and histories, are placed by the bed, near the kitchen, in the car, in my study, down the basement.

Never before at night, at 3 a.m., have I approached you with the complexity of dream language and half-asleep yourself, you say: "The beast . . . the big . . ." And now I am awake enough to wonder that I asked the word, "behemoth," and that you knew the word, "behemoth," and answered.

You, the answering, precise one.
Me, the one who dreamed beyond what I know.

The little lively sparrows light
like a swirl of leaves on the patio.
They are desperately busy
with their daily requirements of food
one-quarter of their weight.
The birds are all pulse and feathers.
They make me tired.

The story of *The Little Engine That Could*
is being read in the next room.
It makes me tired,
all the huffing and puffing.
What we need is to be able
to give up more.
To lay our hands in our laps,
that still of pure absorption:
falling for the world in a way
that we may sit for hours
eyeing things softly
in the delicate manner of light.

Countertops, tables,
book observed as things
apart from their usefulness to us.
In appreciating the geranium,
I see green, I see red.
I notice dried blossoms but leave them.
They are like dust in my room,
the disheveled papers, unanswered letters,
unwashed cups: they are history
not to be tinkered with today.

And then there was the moon,
a shiver of light alone
among the grey and black
shadows of the buttes.

All night long we fell with the stars
lulled by the horse-hoof rhythms
of the cowboys who sang
as they rode along towards Pecos,
Waco, Texas, and Wichita.

The railroad cars coupled
and uncoupled.
Across the range, a whisper.

Then the hills took shape
in the grey-green morning
as they have a million other mornings
with and without crowing,
before and after railroads,
ponies, sagebrush, and us.

On the finger of land
beyond the hours
when humans are allowed,
we stop the car,
listen how the breakers
try to beat their way
out of the harbor.
Never has there been
such loud water,
all sound, no sight.
Finally, a smudge
of grey on black
with small blue lights—
a ship.

Arching back, we see
the skies begin
a pulse of red.
These are signs
of an enormous order.
We make vows of silence
and break them
immediately
to talk for hours
about the primitive,
how we saw inside
the body of the sky.

BREAKFAST

The new kitchen curtains rise with a fat wind of spring.
It is morning, we are stirring up an omelette.
You are playful again. About the tinny sound
of a motorcycle, you say: "Someone is riding
his alarm clock to work."

I like us best like this: humorous, domestic,
having drunk only a little beer,
having gone to bed early, setting our systems
right on the balance between sleep and wakefulness.
We woke on our own.

I want it to be like it is today, always.
But I think about the time the car broke down
and my face was a blister of purple heat,
the time we were rude to each other in front of friends.
And I know I'll bicker with you about how you cook shrimp
and you'll want me to lose five or ten pounds
and play tennis.
My retort will send you spinning.

I continue breaking eggs, slicing mushrooms.
You give me a hug in passing and say:
"I can't get over it." Neither can I,
again and again and again.

EXIT ALONE

Exiting from a movie theatre at 8 p.m.
I stand in front of sheer panes of glass.
Orange tongues of clouds loll on the horizon.
The revelation of orange, of eating and drinking
and going to a film alone: certain colors
are seen only when a person is alone.

I am all alone walking on a city street,
regardless that a man in a VW honks
or a window shade goes down in an apartment
or, right in front of me, a boy falls off his bike
and, like most people who fall, pretends he didn't,
or that he meant to, all along.

Solitude is like bursting out of a house
where we are warm and loved, but sleepy.
Outdoors is sharp blue.
Its smells slap me awake:
catalpa, wet dirt,
the yeasty odor of grain mills,
the old, dark blast of trains.

I stand in the dark chamber
of my house, smell
the heady rot of hyacinths.
They are burning blossom white,
the after-moons of the flash photo.
Still and menacing flowers,
they encroach on the glass boundary
of my angers.

March is tired and grey-hooded.
Even the trees are enemies.
My eyes glaze over as if iced.

Women half my age are holding babies
to the sugar of their breasts.
Summer will see them on park benches
or at K-Mart, tugging along a raised hand
and a small live bundle beneath.

I raise my hand to ask the questions,
I raise my hand to my eyes,
I put my hand in my lap.

Oh, amazed breath that gains its substance
from the cool air,
I can wait for the birds.
I will promise them seeds, heated baths.
Little kings and queens of the southern court,
little arrows,
grace me with your return.

THE OWL OF THE BACK PASTURES

1.

With a wallop a magician
opens a folded top hat
so large the night and its torn pieces
of stars fall in.
Our conversations rise and fall:
Do you call that star Venus?
My father says so. Do you still
climb rocks toward those stars?
Not since my friend died. Now I dance.

2.

Some moonlight caught in a cylinder:
that white finger of tree
peeled clean.
The startled owl startles us.
Lifting from the chimney of tree,
its wings gulping air.
As if darkness swallowed a bit of itself
making the dusk brighter,
the bird's shape burns.
At the moment of takeoff,
all there is is an owl rising,
all gigantic wingspread and fright.
A glide of dun feathers, gone—
a bird of magnitude
living its night life
in the solitary back pastures,
a vanishing act of great beauty.

BIOGRAPHICAL NOTES

Margaret Hasse was born in South Dakota in 1950. After graduating from Stanford University with a B.A. in English, she moved back to the Midwest and now makes her home in Minneapolis.

For ten years she's taught for such programs as Writers in the Schools (COMPAS), the Loft, Minneapolis Community College, and New Focus: Arts in Corrections. She has an M.A. in English (with a writing emphasis) from the University of Minnesota.

Sign of a Child, a collaborative play she wrote with two others, was produced by the Women's Theatre Project in 1982. Recently, she was a featured writer in an innovative theatre production sponsored by the Loft, *Secret Traffic: Four Poets in Performance*.

Currently, she's employed as executive director of Minnesota Alliance for Arts in Education.

Stars Above, Stars Below is her first collection of poems.

THE MINNESOTA VOICES PROJECT

#18 Neal Bowers, THE GOLF BALL DIVER (poems), $3.50

Jonis Agee, and others, eds. BORDER CROSSINGS: A MINNESOTA VOICES PROJECT READER, $8.00

The Fourth Annual Competition

#19 Margaret Hasse, STARS ABOVE, STARS BELOW (poems), $3.50

#20 C. J. Hribal, MATTY'S HEART (short stories) $6.00

#21 Sheryle Noethe, THE DESCENT OF HEAVEN OVER THE LAKE (poems), $3.50

#22 Monica Ochtrup, WHAT I CANNOT SAY/I WILL SAY (poems) $3.50

Copies of any or all of these books may be purchased directly from the publisher by filling out the coupons below and mailing it, together with a check for the correct amount and $1.00 per order for postage and handling, to:

New Rivers Press
1602 Selby Ave.
St. Paul, MN 55104

Please send me the following books: _____

_____

_____

_____

_____

_____

I am enclosing $_____ (which includes $1.00 for postage and handling)
Please send these books as soon as possible to:

NAME _____

ADDRESS _____

CITY & STATE _____

ZIP _____